Touring

poems by

Marjie Giffin

Finishing Line Press
Georgetown, Kentucky

Touring

Copyright © 2021 by Marjie Giffin
ISBN 978-1-64662-410-2 First Edition
All rights reserved under International and Pan-American Copyright Conventions. No part of this book may be reproduced in any manner whatsoever without written permission from the publisher, except in the case of brief quotations embodied in critical articles and reviews.

ACKNOWLEDGMENTS

"Back in '73" first appeared in *Blue Heron Review*
"Backseat Rider," "Goodwill," "Mother's Company," and "Place of Peace" first appeared in *Flying Island*
"Brattle Street" first appeared in *So It Goes: The Journal of the Kurt Vonnegut Memorial Library, No. 6*
"Empty City" first appeared in *Tipton Poetry Journal*
"Hondo, New Mexico" first appeared in *St. Katherine Review*
"The Plunge" first appeared in *Snapdragon: A Journal of Art and Healing*
"The Potted Plant" first appeared in *So It Goes: The Journal of the Kurt Vonnegut Memorial Library, No. 7*
"The Refugee" first appeared in *The Lives We Live(d) In: An Anthology of Poems about Social Justice*
"Stillness" first appeared in *Poetry Quarterly*
"Touring" first appeared in *Northwest Indiana Literary Journal*

Publisher: Leah Huete de Maines
Editor: Christen Kincaid
Cover Art: Marjie Giffin
Author Photo: Jason M. Kelly
Cover Design: Elizabeth Maines McCleavy

Order online: www.finishinglinepress.com
also available on amazon.com

Author inquiries and mail orders:
Finishing Line Press
PO Box 1626
Georgetown, Kentucky 40324
USA

Table of Contents

Spring Break 1

Dead End 2

Fire Nights 3

Brattle Street 4

Touring 5

The Plunge 6

Hondo, New Mexico 7

Back in '73 8

The Refugee 9

Backseat Rider 10

Goodwill 12

Earth Day 13

Mother's Company 14

Birthday Greetings 15

The Potted Plant 16

The Church in Milwaukee 18

My Way with Water 19

North to Ann Arbor 20

Place of Peace 21

The Masses 22

Stillness 23

Girls Trip 25

Sanibel 26

Grandbaby 27

A Flight of Fancy 28

Empty City 29

Dedicated to Christopher, Matthew, and Elisabeth

Spring Break

begins with so much banter
about which beach towns,
which coast, which caravan
each family is bound to follow.
Lockers clang shut as kids trip
all over their feet to careen
down the halls to waiting cars.
The sweaty air is electric
with excitement as shouts
go up and hasty goodbyes
are exchanged. Lost amid
the hoopla are the kids
who will pen their "What I Did
Over Spring Break" essays
with more muted enthusiasm:
I stayed overnight with my Nana,
or *I got to visit my Dad,*
or *Mostly I felt real hungry.*

Dead End

A fishy, foul smell rose from the rocks below
and a few eye-balling carcasses lay spread flat
where the water lapped up against the pilings.

Two grizzled guys loitered by the cars parked
in the five or six spaces allotted for the public.
An unmistakable Brooklyn accent cut the quiet.

I squinted, trying to shut out the tawdry scene
and focus on the crystalline blue water, the sails—
an Impressionist painting spread across my mind.

Behind me, the yellow canopies of a yacht club
rippled in the soft June breeze and tinkling sounds
of glassware and conversation wafted on the air.

This spot was the Dead End marked on the sign
that signaled outsiders to turn back, conveyed
notice that this was private, privileged ground

except for the small, squat parking lot reserved
for the lucky few who drove in early enough
to secure the cheap seats for a view of the bay.

And so the glimmering sea held my gaze, sure
as I was that Greenwich's cozy access should
not be denied me, a mere traveler on my way.

Fire Nights

Nights so hot we slept on swept cement,
toes touching as we star-gazed from the
    rail-rimmed porch.

Secrets scurried back and forth and whispers
teased the air while fireflies flitted above
    our upturned faces.

Voices drifted and ice cubes clinked while
neighbors shifted sticky bodies about on
    aluminum lawn chairs.

Breezeless nights, stagnant nights,
nights as still as the gnats and mosquitoes
    that bit us wordlessly
    and without warning.

And sometimes Fire Nights, when sirens would wail
and the family would pile into the silent Chevy
    and cruise the streets and
    follow the haze

and find the Fire and watch agape at
the licking fingers that leapt and danced
and scorched the walls and sizzled the halls
    until we could watch no more.

And then home we turned and cruised again
and sniffed the air and smelled our hair
    to see if the Fire Night
    was still with us, there.

Brattle Street

I butt my head against a gust of biting wind
and let my crimson scarf whip across my face
and blind me to the ragged heap in front of me.

What the hell? I want to shout—*It's Harvard Square!*
as I dodge shapeless forms that dot the icy sidewalks,
humps and mounds slumped under faded wraps.

Nearby at The Charles, the lobby exudes warmth
as gushing alums crush one another, arms outstretched
and checkbooks open to embrace their alma mater.

Inside hallowed classrooms and well-endowed labs,
great minds from across the globe converge and converse,
tilting heads together to brainstorm and save the world.

On Brattle Street, students trudge through soot and slush,
intent in their pursuit of the higher arts and sciences,
resolved to right the wrongs and injustices that blight us.

Past fast food joints, coffee shops, bookstores, and pubs—
Harvard thinkers plod on and on, sidestepping the bodies
that so artlessly litter the landscape, block their progress.

I shake the snow from my scarf as I climb into a cab—
take one last look as we pull from the curb. Some clumps
move, some stay still, and I have no diploma to explain it.

Touring

More than the rules of the game,
I remember the setting: the blonde
dining table, the street light shining
through the sheer curtains, the jade
ash tray collecting dirty cigar stubs.
Coke bottles littering the four corners,
popcorn kernels strewn in a haphazard
way. Dad seated at the head of the table,
presiding. An old sea dog, *Captain
of the Pacific Fleet.* He who had dealt
many rounds of cards in the bowels
of the *New Mexico* battleship must
have found our family coterie quite tame.
Yet we were delighted to have his
attention, a rare thing. There he sat,
Cutty Sark at his elbow, *El Camino*
crunched in the corner of his mouth,
angling for another gasoline card—
the card that kept you on the road.
That was the aim of the game, I
remember—to keep the engine going,
to keep touring the country, back when
WWII guys like Dad thought a drive
on an open road equaled the freedom
for which they had risked their lives.

The Plunge

I am running out of time
but I'd like to slip down
the mossy steps
of my sister's pier
and plunge headfirst
without hesitation
into the still-chilled June waters
of her pristine Northern lake
and push off the stony bottom
and float and float and float—
perhaps as far as Canada—
where wild geese, arching,
would flap down at me
as I churned my aging body
forward and they would circle,
nodding, bestowing their respect.

Hondo, New Mexico

Hondo has packed up and left.
Scrub grass, dry leaves, heat remain.
A dilapidated frame building leans
toward the dusty road as we slow
to peer: U.S. Post Office. A sepia wash
colors the setting with soft
tones of brown and stucco reds.

Vivid doesn't thrive in Hondo.
Yet the Southwestern sun still
glitters against the faded scene.
Tumbleweed skitters past us,
the only motion besides the sweep
of wind, muted sighs—sounds
of ghosts who once awaited mail.

Back in '73

Back in '73, he was "killing me softly
with his song," and I was longing
to be his bride. With car idling
by the lake, old motor humming,
he crooned and stroked my cheek
and promised me the moon
would beam down on us forever.

I traced continents all across his back,
and he found hints of the sea
in the green flecks of my eyes.
We traveled sitting still, slept and
awakened, wondering at the expanse
of places that neither of us
had ever before seen.

The hush of the woods
enveloped us, and we were alone
in our vast but secluded world.
We vowed always to be explorers,
always to probe finger and toe
all those regions yet unknown
to our most tender touch.

Like an unspoken promise,
the honeyed stillness lulled us
into a thrill for the uncharted
and a faith in our own magic
to conquer ocean, plain, and sky.
Time was a blur, and we let loose
our dreams, and for one
singing moment, we believed.

The Refugee

The way was long and hard, hot and dry,
and she yearned for *agua* to slake the thirst and wet
her cracked lips that stuck together—soothe the roof
of her mouth that was veined like thin parchment.
Caravan connotes a train of vehicles, some transport
other than grimy feet, caked with dust and mud
and throbbing so heavily that she could hear the plodding
of each footfall in her ears as she trudged forward.

Yet the caravan of which so many expressed fear
was just the mass of them, refugees from far-away places
where danger lurks in every doorway, where drugs
are the currency in which their children must trade. They
could not turn back, no matter the threat, for a last breath
behind them was more certain than whispered death ahead.

Backseat Rider

Crammed into the backseat
of my offspring's shiny new SUV
with two lifejackets, a sack
of boxed cookies, a carton full
of tri-colored tissue-wrapped gifts,
my hefty purse, extra tennis shoes,
and this notebook, I scribble.

I contemplate my destiny:
relegation to the backseat
for the rest of my days.
I now have senior status
which, translated, means
I pay for gas and hotel rooms
and stops for burgers and fries,
and I sit forever in the back
with the baggage.

I have brought too much stuff,
my suitcase weighs too much,
my head is in the way
of my in-law's rearview mirror.

I need too many bathroom stops,
my phone volume is set too loud,
I forgot to bring the correct change
for the trail of toll booths.

My varicose veins throb
due to my crumpled position,
and my neck aches from bending
my head out of sight.

I dare not complain, or I will be
stereotyped as a crabby old biddy—
anything I say can so easily
be turned against me.

Up front, the radio is dialed
to their station, the cup holders
are filled with their drinks,
and there, the leg-room is ample.

Back here, I chafe away at my age
and suddenly understand my mother
so much better than I did when, years
before, I assigned her to the same seat.

Goodwill

is scattered all over the canopied bay
among the trampled cardboard boxes
and crumpled bags and soggy sheets.
A young, moody-faced teen languishes
on the curb, nodding when spoken to
but not answering my motion for help.
Figures, I think, cursing lazy youth,
as I trot to the back of my car and heave
up the hatch and begin loading my arms
with all the added goodwill I can muster:
baubles that came from Macy's, canisters
that once spilled out Gold Medal flour,
baby dolls that were kissed and held.
No time for sentiment; tepid rain drips
from the awning and pools on cracked,
uneven cement. The scent of moldy
cast-offs mixes with the mustiness
of tentative, springtime rain. A sack
of Christmas candies catches the eye
of the non-attentive teen; *May I?*
his eyes seem to ask. I toss it to him
like a bridal bouquet. In the rearview
mirror as I pull away, I see him grinning
as he digs in the crinkly, silver sack.

Earth Day

The wise say forest bathing is therapeutic,
the cool, calm air whispering between trees
a balm for the tired, the worried, the worn.

Ocean breezes also soothe the soul; sand oozing
between the toes eases tension, and feet splashing
in the surf create a splattering, laughing sound.

The views from a high mountain vista
are sweeping and bold; wispy clouds clamor
to be touched as they skim the sky around them.

In nature we find both solace and solution.
Little can we afford to abandon Earth's allure,
our calling to save it most crucial and assured.

Mother's Company

Mother is having company.

It's been years, but I still recall
turkey platters and gilded plates,
soup tureens with china ladles,
crystal stemware and cubes of ice
that clinked together musically.

There were lavender-scented soaps
tucked amidst lacey table linens
in drawers so laden with heirlooms
that Mother would strain to pull
their polished, glistening handles.

I could breathe in and catch
the scent of Chanel No. 5;
I would steal a peek and see
her lips pursed before the glass
as she coated them with red.

Today's company is being served
on paper plates on a kitchen table
so crammed with paraphernalia
that the tasteless sandwiches
almost tip off its edge.

Photos, stacks of letters, nail files,
coupon boxes, hosiery eggs—
all compete for centerpiece space
and the attention of the
curious guests who dine.

One of the favored few shaves
with an electric razor in between
snatches of conversation, bites.
Another, his wife, balances her plate
protectively between two dry elbows.

I make clever talk with both, knowing
there will be hours later for despair.

Birthday Greetings

Honk! It's Charley's Birthday!—
the vivid sign caught my eye
as I sped along a leafy side street,
my mind still numb from lack
of coffee and too little sleep
from the night before. With bold
letters splashed across cardboard
in primary colors, the celebratory sign
spelled devotion in unspoken detail.
In my mind's eye as I peered
down the roadway, I pictured
a doting mom canvassing a house
for cardboard and paints—a handy
dad poring over the project
so that (likely) little Charley
would be feted with honks galore.
Inwardly grinning, I imagined
a delighted Charley peering through
a handsomely-draped window,
busily counting car beeps on
stubby little fingers and toes.
Happy Birthday, Charley! I spoke
aloud, glad for any small guy
who inspired so much love.

The Potted Plant

His parents sent a potted plant.
How did they not drive frantically
from Arkansas when learning
their son was bunking on a mattress
in a hospital psychiatric ward?

White coats took his keys, razor, and comb.
They left the potted plant alone.
When he talked to me on visits,
his eyes darted nervously.
I wasn't sure he knew who I was.

I was still his fiancé early on.
But the chaplain said he understood.
He said I couldn't be sure
of *what might lie ahead,*
so he absolved me of my guilt.

My own father drove down—
said he wanted to see for himself.
He saw that there were no
keys or razors or combs.
I'm sure he noted the potted plant.

Then my father, too, released me:
It's not anything you could have foreseen.
Of course not. No giddy bride-to-be
anticipates a dark walk down an antiseptic
hallway into a room full of *no things*.

No things. No framed photographs.
Can't take chances with glass, of course.
No wallet or driver's license.
Can't leave the premises, of course.
No parents, but there sat the surrogate plant.

And then, no fiancé. Because that had been me.
Before the betrothed became a stranger.
Before the white coats took all his things.
Before the writing blazed upon the wall.
Before I wept over a wilted potted plant.

The Church in Milwaukee

sat, imposing, near the Lake
Michigan waterfront on grounds
composed of cement and grass.
Catholic, it rose high above a
stack of battered steps, cracked
and worn by pilgrims seeking
worship and peace across the
years. We trudged up the steps,
our shoulders hunched against
a biting wind under slate winter
skies. Milling around its heavy
wooden doors, bedraggled men
and women begged for the charity
of church-goers on that cold,
merciless day. Voices mingled,
murmuring, hoping for visitors
who would share. One woman,
slouching in a shapeless coat,
inched shyly forward, her
head uncovered—hands stuffed
in pockets—face ashen with cold.
Shaking, we fumbled in our laden
purses, but as she pulled hands
from empty pockets, our eyes
froze on her missing fingers;
frostbite, she mouthed in barely
audible words. On instinct, my
daughter pulled her scarf from
her neck and her hat from her
head as I ripped my gloves from
my hands. We gave what we
could, but it would never be
enough to diminish our sorrow
for our human sister on that
brutal and icy Milwaukee day.

My Way with Water

Water freed me. Goggles hid
my wavering eyes; in the froth
my body achieved form and grace.
I was fast! My reach was strong
and my kick was steady, and I
sped down my lane like a bow
to its mark. How I loved the
joy of being one with the water;
how I loved belonging when
on land I felt unfit. In the foam,
in the slap of the wake I created,
I felt the power of being at home.

North to Ann Arbor

The long car trip of five hours in those days
that seemed to stretch off the edge of the planet

now appears in my memory as almost a lark,
a trip I'd gladly go back in time and retake.

My dad at the wheel in his camel wool coat,
cigar smoke swirling around his head and ours,

a lover of the open road and maps and journeys
and diviner of medical marvels to repair my eyes.

Often we traveled to Ann Arbor and back—
every six weeks for surgeries and post ops

and checkups until, years later, I found my way
to the medical center just by pointing

at which turns to take and which stops to make
until we reached the hill of my memories

where the hospital loomed—perched mightily—
and antiseptic smells permeated my mind.

And what a gift, a sacrifice, on my parents' part
to cram into that car and follow that route

faithfully, countless times, just to unload and sit
and wait in crowded ante-rooms and dank motels

so that I, their firstborn, could have the advantages
of cutting edge science and clear-cut sight.

Place of Peace

Elisabeth sleeps,
knees curled against my groin,
my knees tucked around her toes,
my mother body encircling
her daughter body—
warming the nest,
lining the nest—nesting.

Our cheeks pressed,
her breaths puff evenly,
play a soft cadence
against my skin.
The space between us
is moist and close; a
flutter of her tiny lashes
touches, tickles lightly.

Nestled as we are,
her slumber becoming
my poetry, I commit
the feel of this little one's
life song to memory—
that I might at any moment
recreate this place of peace.

The Masses

Hands clasped, I wedge myself into the line
that snakes slowly toward the Host.

My eyes fasten on the ancient man
whose bent body blocks my way in the aisle.

He is praying, and *rigor mortis* seems to have set in.
I note mottled hands and tightly clenched fists.

A special urgency grips his pleas—
the old man *squeezes* out his prayer to God.

Another elderly couple has kneeled nearby;
their hands are twin steeples, side by side.

Their eyes are closed, heads bowed—
even their lips murmur in unison.

One crinkled lady can't stoop to pray;
another dabs absently at pooling tears.

Burmese children receive pats on their brows,
too young for either the wafer or wine.

Father's rich African accent rings up ahead:
"The body of Christ" feeds many tongues.

I look up above and see Christ peering down,
his near-naked form catching light from the sun.

Lovingly carved and carefully hung,
this teakwood Christ absorbs our pain.

Lined faces, creased and tired, show all around,
as do torn, faded jeans and muddied shoes.

The masses are worn, beaten; many are down.
Hearts weigh heavy, souls seek to be found.

Stillness

It is late in the night
and I wander.

        The bookcases stand silent,
        ends like good soldiers
        guarding the tomes
        and all the sacred words.

        The piano sits grandly,
        keys glistening in darkness,
        sheet music strewn
        artlessly, no sounds aroused.

        Ice-streaked panes reflect light
        from the shimmering snow
        and the sole table lamp
        and the porch light's glow.

I feel transformed
by a holy stillness.

        The lake is glassy and deep in hue.
        Trees like sentinels line its shore
        and in their upright bearing
        give stark outline to the frozen scene.

        The snow piled round the house
        rises and falls in softer folds
        and sparkles where glints of light
        dazzle its closer mounds.

        The sky rises high and mightily.
        Frothy clouds seem to waft among
        winking stars and skim by
        winter's wafer-like moon.

My breathing slows.
I close my eyes.
Is this therapy or prayer?
Stillness—balm for the soul.
I wish to keep myself there.

Girls Trip

I hoist my purple duffle up into the Range Rover
amidst the carton of Corona Lights and the paper sacks
full of crackers and protein bars and Gala apples
and the laundry basket heaped with friend Kassie's
clothes, laptop, paperbacks, and bags of chocolate bark.

The four of us head north, heavy laden among truck
traffic—semis and car trailers and pick-ups all wearing
down their treads and rutting the roadway between
Indy and Chi-town—and pause halfway there to gawk
at wind farm arms generating power across the Plains.

Exuberant with girl power, we, too, can spin and whirl
on the Lake Michigan shore and romp free among
the rocks and stoop to collect stones, pondering
if prehistoric or washed to us from distant lands whose
lore we can only stare across waves to conjure.

Escaping from the humdrum of our author lives—
blending the pleasure of lattes, bagels, and wine
with the torturous search for words so precise—
we bask in the early autumn sun on the beach
and then stretch out hearthside to whisper at night.

The following day, storms roll in across the water,
and we carry in logs to keep dry for the fire.
Modern electronics mix with the musty, earthy
environs of the rustic cabin hidden in the trees.
We type furiously with blankets 'round our knees.

The family of deer that grazes out the window
charms us, while a chatter-bugging chipmunk
breaks the spell. Who knows what works nature
will arouse in us, if any at all? Yet we absorb
the spirit of things—the lake, the woods, the call.

Sanibel
Post Hurricane Charley

Sleepy,
she lolls on the shore,
tickled by thousands
of tiny shells, trimmed
out in glossy trains
of tangled seaweed.

Lazy,
she seldom shifts her pose,
basks contentedly
by the beach
and slumbers airily
to ocean lullabies.

Protective,
she guards her secrets,
coy as she courts
discerning travelers
but firm in her
defensive stance.

Wistful,
she yearns for bygone years
when time stood still
and roads were paths
and locals kept
their solitary watch
by the shimmering sea.

Tested,
she has weathered
the worst of Nature's wrath
and, never vanquished,
has searched her soul
and found the strength
to rise again, survive.

Grandbaby
For Bailee Anne

I greet you with bliss and yet
misgivings: you who are of me
and of my child and who bear
resemblance even to those
who gave birth before me.
All I want to do is hold you
and enfold you and brand
you with soft kisses.
I could count your toes
to eternity—press noses
till they thought us Eskimos.
But you are not mine alone,
and I'm called to pass you
like a gift to be admired.
You are to be a shared gift;
we are all to be the richer.
Yet when my turn is over,
I'll tuck you in my heart.

A Flight of Fancy

The lives I didn't lead sometimes bewitch me.
Wondering where I might have gone or who
I might have been . . . contemplating the great
               Other.

When I'm restless, my mind travels West
to the mighty Tetons, where I visited once
and was struck almost dumb by the
majesty of the peaks and the green vistas.

In Italy, on a soft-lit evening on a piazza
in Venice, I pretended I was a local,
out for a stroll in my own environs,
belonging and blending in, at home.

Once, when I owned a small escape
on a barrier island called Sanibel, I
mused that I might settle in there, sand
beneath my feet, and stay a long while.

Might I have wings like an eagle soaring,
I would dip down to eye such spots,
take a flight of fancy, so to speak,
and for a brief moment, transform myself
               into Another.

Empty City

The people have all gone inside;
the sounds of the city have died
and a soft silence like snow has fallen
all over the street lamps and crossings
and benches where talking has ceased.

The co-mingling is missed, the scurry
of hurrying people and the lost tempo
of traffic—the rhythms of urban life.
A dullness descends, unspoken grief
at a place, still and mute, that once cried

out for our notice, for caution in face
of a stealthy foe, an illness creeping
on a cat's sly paws down our sidewalks
and up stairways and even across
lawns at our city's outer-most edge.

Paying little heed, we now pay a price
for our complacency, our nod of heads
at notions of sneaking death, as if we
could little comprehend the need
to rouse ourselves from quiet stupor.

So now the emptiness prevails, and
wails are all that can be heard, and sighs
that waft down among the shadows
from balconies and rooftops of a city
that has gathered itself inside, alone.

Author's Note

Thanks to all readers for taking the time to read these pages. I'd also like to thank a long-ago mentor, Marianne Darr Norman, who gave me my earliest encouragement as a writer and who exemplified how to teach critical thinking skills; my longtime friend and source of guidance on all of life's thorny issues, Gloria Vasquez; and my writer son-in-law and daughter, Christopher and Elisabeth Speckman, for their helpful acts of patience and assistance in all things technical and for their abiding good taste. Nods of gratitude also go to my writing colleagues of seven years: Kassie Ritman, Enid Cokinos, and Judy Miller, and to the excellent former instructors who read my manuscript with complimentary responses, Shari Wagner and Kyle Craig.

Marjie Giffin
Summer 2020

Marjie Giffin is a Midwestern writer who resides in Indianapolis, where she is active in the Indiana Writers Center. Her collegiate years were spent on the campus of Indiana University in Bloomington, Indiana, and later in Indianapolis, where she earned an M.A. in English from Butler University. She also pursued certification in gifted and talented education from Indiana University-Purdue University, Indianapolis, and has taught both college-level writing and middle school gifted education.

Early in her career, Marjie focused on regional history, and four of her works were commissioned: *Water Runs Downhill*, *If Tables Could Talk*, *A Walk Through Time*, and an abbreviated history for the Newcomen Association. She also co-authored *A Middle School Guide to Literary Terms* with another colleague, Mary Ann Yedinak.

Marjie has also dabbled in playwriting and had her 10-minute play, *The Send Off*, produced in the IndyFringe Short Play Festival. Her poetry has recently been published in *So It Goes: the Kurt Vonnegut Literary Journal*; *Northwest Indiana Literary Journal*; *Flying Island*; *Tipton Poetry Journal*; *Blue Heron Review*; *St. Katherine Review*; *Snapdragon: A Journal of Healing and Art*; *Through the Sycamores*; *Poetry Quarterly*; *The World We Live(d) In: An Anthology of Poems about Social Justice*; and *What Was and Will Be: Life in the Time of COVID-19*.

Free time for Marjie includes time spent with her family as well as time spent reading, writing, traveling, and communing with three author friends in their bi-weekly writing workshop.

www.ingramcontent.com/pod-product-compliance
Lightning Source LLC
LaVergne TN
LVHW041510070426
835507LV00012B/1454